Penguin
Random
House

Recipe Writer and Food Stylist
Kate Turner

Writer and Editor Ruth O'Rourke-Jones

Project Art Editor Harriet Yeomans

Editorial Assistant Alice Horne

Design Assistance
Jade Wheaton, Alison Gardner

Jacket Designer Harriet Yeomans

Jacket Coordinator Libby Brown

Pre-production Producer
Rob Dunn

Print Producer Stephanie McConnell

Creative Technical Support
Sonia Charbonnier

Photography Will Heap

Managing Editor Dawn Henderson

Managing Art Editor
Marianne Markham

Art Director Maxine Pedliham

Publishing Director Mary-Clare Jerram

First published in Great Britain in 2017
By Dorling Kindersley Limited,
80 Strand, London WC2R 0RL

Copyright © 2017 Dorling Kindersley

A Penguin Random House Company

2 4 6 8 10 9 7 5 3 1
001 – 304992 – Jan/2017

ISBN: 978-0-2412-9652-3

Printed and bound in China

A WORLD OF IDEAS:
SEE ALL THERE IS TO KNOW

www.dk.com

MY
ZERO-
WASTE
KITCHEN

Contents

NOW ZERO-WASTE IT!

Zero waste:
what's it all about?

Going "zero waste" means trying to live a more sustainable life. It is a goal to aspire to and your kitchen is the perfect place to start. Having a zero-waste kitchen means buying less food in the first place, reusing whatever you can, however you can, and throwing less away. Don't worry, you won't have to completely overhaul your whole lifestyle – in fact, you might just be surprised at the big difference some small, simple changes can make. From planning your food shop to what you put on your plate,

this book is full of amazing tips and tricks to help you get creative, start reducing waste, and even have fun doing it!

The three "Rs"

Key to zero-waste living are the three "Rs":

REDUCE • REUSE • RECYCLE

"Reduce" means not buying more than you need and this is where a little planning goes a long way. "Reuse" means making the most of those leftovers rather than binning them. With

Swap-it
Smoothie p12

Creative
Crisps p46

Hero
Hummus p20

a bit of thought and inspiration you can turn your "waste" foods into delicious meals that are good for you, for your purse, and for the planet! Try the recipes in this book as a starting point and soon you'll be experimenting with whatever you have to hand. Lastly, "recycle" anything that you can't reduce or reuse. Throughout this book you'll find inspirational, easy, and imaginative ways to put all these ideas into practice and help you on your zero-waste journey.

shake up
your cake p58

" *A few* small **changes** *can* *make a* **big** *difference.* "

Getting started:
no more waste!

*Going **ZERO-WASTE** is easy – with a little thought and planning you'll soon be on your way. Stopping to consider **WHAT** you throw away and **WHY** is the best place to start.*

STOP! *BEFORE YOU BANISH THAT "WASTE" TO THE BIN, ASK YOURSELF...*

CAN YOU EAT IT? — NO → **CAN YOU REUSE IT?** — NO

YES

Eat and enjoy!
You might be surprised – lots of things we throw away are edible (see pp.28–29).

YES

So use it again!
Many kitchen items can be revived, reused, or repurposed (see pp.68–69).

Foil trays

Dry-cured meats

Hard cheese

ALL DONE!

CLEVER COMPOSTING

Composting is one of the best ways to go zero-waste. It puts the energy that goes into producing food back into the soil in your garden. In a compost bin, microbes use air and water to break down organic matter into nutrient-rich dirt.

All you need is a bin that lets air circulate. Start with a leaf layer (shredded paper will do), then add fruit and veg scraps, and water. Add to your compost all year round. Stir it occasionally and in 8–9 months you'll have natural fertilizer.

A counter-top composter helps you compost as much as you can. Put scraps into your mini composter through the week and add them to your garden compost once it's full. Use a proper container to avoid attracting flies into your kitchen!

Counter-top composter

CAN YOU COMPOST IT?

NO →

CAN YOU RECYCLE IT?

NO →

YES

Add to your composter.
You can compost much more than you may realize!
(see pp.16–17)!

Scraps

YES

Put it in the recycling bin.
Up to 60 per cent of waste that ends up in landfill could have been recycled! Check before you chuck!

Recycling bin

THROW IT IN THE BIN.

YOU'RE A WASTE-FREE WINNER!

Store it right!

*Storing your produce in the **RIGHT WAY** can be the difference between*
***MAKING THE MOST** of your food and throwing it **OUT**.*

Where should I store it?

Check labels when you put your shopping away as many products carry storage instructions.

Once opened, some items need to go in the fridge (see p.48) and be used within a few days, so note when you open the pack. Store salad items and leafy greens in the salad drawer of your fridge. If your fruits need to ripen before eating, don't chill them, leave them out in a fruit bowl until they are ready. Your kitchen cupboard is great for shutting out light so keep spices, oils, and some veg – such as onions and root vegetables – dry and dark, in here.

What should I put it in?

Reusable containers do a great job at cutting down waste.

Using the right containers keeps your food in tip-top condition for as long as possible. Transfer dried goods, such as spices or pasta and rice, to air-tight glass, or ceramic jars to keep them fresh for six months or more. While plastic is easy to carry around for food-on-the-go, it should only be used for cold food, as high tempertaures can cause it to break down. In the fridge, keep asparagus, cucumber, carrots, and celery fresh by popping them upright in a jar of water.

Super tip

Stop garlic spoiling by tying bulbs into tights. Then hang them up!

Be prepared!

With a little prep, some foods can be stored for much longer.

Blanching vegetables, such as green beans, before freezing them not only makes them last longer but also brightens their colour and slows nutrient loss. Pop them in the freezer on a baking sheet then transfer to an airtight container – they will keep for up to 10 months.

Drying vegetables, such as onions and chillies, for storage is easy. Use a dehydrator (see right) for fleshy chillies. For waxy varieties, wash them in salt water, then pop them on a wire rack in a warm, dry spot – a windowsill is good. In a few weeks you will have a batch of dried chillies.

Airtight containers keep food fresh and dry.

A LiTTLE EXTRA HELP...

You don't need to use fancy gadgets and gizmos to go zero-waste but some ingenious inventions can help.

- **A dehydrator** is handy for preserving fruit, veg, herbs, and even meat. It gently dries food out while preserving nutrients and flavour.

- **Vacuum-packing** your food preserves freshness by removing air and saves valuable space.

- **A cut-herb keeper** will help your herbs stay fresher for longer by suspending them in water.

Cut-herb keeper

Swap-it Smoothie

From APPLE CORES to KIWI SKINS and LEFTOVER GREENS, this nutrient-packed smoothie gets the most out of your fruit and veg.

SERVES 2

120g (4¼oz) fresh strawberries

120g (4¼oz) frozen berries, such as blueberries and raspberries

350ml (12fl oz) nut milk, such as almond milk

35g (1¼oz) oats

2 tbsp seeds, such as hemp, chia, sesame, or flax, plus extra to garnish (optional)

1 tbsp raw honey, plus extra to taste

FIRST **MAKE THE BASE**

1 Place all the ingredients in a high-speed blender and whizz until smooth.

2 Add extra honey to taste and pour the smoothie into glasses to serve. Sprinkle with extra seeds to garnish, if using.

Super tip
There's no need to hull the strawberries – just add them in whole.

KIWI AND BANANA WITH SKINS

To the base recipe, add **1 small banana – about 75g (2½oz)** – with the skin on but tough ends removed, and **half a kiwi – about 50g (1¾oz)** – with the skin on.

LEFTOVER GREENS

Add about **2 handfuls of leftover greens** such as chopped kale stalks, broccoli stems and leaves, celery tops and tails, lettuce, spinach, or avocado, to the base recipe.

OLD APPLES AND CORES

Add **1 medium unpeeled apple or apple cores – about 120g (4¼oz)** – to the base recipe. Remove the tough stalk, but keep the pips.

Zero-waste week

*Planning ahead can make the difference between a **WASTEFUL WEEK** and a **WASTE-FREE ONE**. Follow these simple pointers to help you on your way.*

PLAN YOUR MEALS

Life gets in the way of the best-laid plans. If you struggle to stick to a strict meal plan, you could try planning your meals more loosely. This makes it easy to adapt as plans change. Having space to vary meals makes shopping easier and you should waste less. Consider basing your week's evening meals around a type of food, such as pasta, fish, or grains (see meal plan, right). That way you can stretch ingredients across a few meals, work in what you have to hand, or what you fancy on the day.

MEAL PLAN

Monday	Tuesday	Wednesday
RICE	**DOUGH**	**LEGUMES**
• stir-fry	• pizza	• soups
• risotto	• pie	• stews
• paella	• quiche	• casseroles
• chilli	• fajitas	
• curry		

Friday	Saturday	Sunday
FISH	**GO OFF PLAN!**	**MEAT AND/OR GRAINS**
• with any veg and mashed, boiled, or chipped potatoes	• eat out	• Sunday roast
	• invite friends for dinner	• grain-based loaf and salad
	• try something new	

RICE - chicken and pancetta risotto

FISH - Add veg and potatoes

DOUGH - Salmon and spinach quiche

Roast
chicken

Roasted
vegetables

iNVOLVE EVERYONE

When it comes to planning meals for the week, get everybody involved from the start. List meals that everyone in your household enjoys and make that your starting point. You are all far more likely to stick to a meal plan that you feel enthusiastic about. You can vary the meals by working in leftovers and whatever you have to hand.

Thursday

PASTA
- with whatever you have in your veg drawer
- with herby pesto

LEFTOVER LUNCHES

When planning your dinners think about how you can use leftovers in lunches. Rather than reheating the same meals, give them a new spin. Spoon yesterday's chilli into wraps, turn last night's pasta into a salad, or layer up leftovers into a lunch pot.

- Bean sprouts
- Hummus
- Beetroot
- Peas
- Boiled egg
- Red peppers
- Spinach
- Brown rice

PASTA - Leftover veg

BREAK iT DOWN

You might find that planning and shopping for a whole week's worth of food doesn't work for you. If you find it hard to stick to a plan or you are wasting food towards the end of the week, try breaking your week down into a three- or four-day plan instead. Then devote the following day to making meals from any leftovers you have.

LEGUMES -
Bean and pumpkin soup

10 things you didn't know you could... COMPOST

CUPCAKE CASES

Paper cupcake or muffin cases can be added to your compost heap where they will break down quickly. Do watch out for any waxy-feeling cases that may contain an element of plastic, which you shouldn't compost. If in doubt, leave it out!

STALE SNACK FOODS

Old crisps, crackers, and biscuits will break down fast in a compost heap, but be sure to bury them deep within the heap as they can attract unwanted visitors to your garden.

CARDBOARD

You might be used to recycling your unwanted cardboard packaging – such as egg and cereal boxes, and toilet and kitchen roll tubes – but did you know that you can rip them up and add them to your compost heap?

TISSUES AND NAPKINS

Paper tissues and napkins will break down quickly in compost. Do consider what they have been used for though. If you've been unwell and used tissues to blow your nose, for example, don't compost them as you could be adding germs to your compost.

SPICES AND HERBS

Old spices and herbs that have lost their smell and flavour can be an extra addition to your compost heap.

Your humble compost heap is full of hidden surprises! Not only can it turn your unwanted **VEGETABLE PEELINGS** into **NUTRIENT-RICH FERTILIZER**, it also works wonders with a whole host of other kitchen waste.

Super tip

keep your compost balanced with an equal mix of soft, green material and drier, brown material.

WINE CORKS

Don't bin that cork once you've popped it! Cork is a natural product that can be added to compost. Do watch out for synthetic corks that have been made to look like the real thing though – plastic will not break down in your compost heap.

CHEWING GUM

Whether you've chewed natural plant-based gum or a synthetic gum, both can be added to your compost. It will take a while to break down but will eventually biodegrade.

WINE AND BEER

Don't pour sour wine or flat beer down the sink, they are great for compost. Both are rich in nitrogen and beer contains yeast for good microbes to feast on. Keep an eye on the moisture levels of your compost, if it's dry then add the liquids but if it's wet add dry material too, such as shredded paper, to balance it out.

DAIRY PRODUCTS

Old milk, cream, and melted ice cream can be added to your compost in small amounts. Take care to bury them deep in your heap as they may attract pests. Mix them well with plenty of leaves to trap any odours and keep your compost balanced.

COTTON TEA TOWELS AND CLOTHS

Cloths or towels that are made from 100 per cent natural fibres, such as cotton or linen, can be composted. Tear them into scraps to help them break down more quickly, but they may still take a while.

17

Veg drawer clear-out

*Faced with a drawer full of **VEGGIES THAT NEED USING FAST?** Fear not, they won't go to waste if you follow these handy hints.*

SALAD LEAVES

- **Pop salad greens** into a pan and sauté them as part of a stir-fry. This works well even if your leaves are a little wilted.

- **Whizz tired leaves** into soups or smoothies for an extra dose of vitamins!

ROOT VEG

- **Roast batches** of mixed root veg and freeze or use them in soups and stews to stock your freezer.

TOMATOES

- **Add fresh tomatoes** that are past their best to soups and pasta sauce, which both freeze well.

- **Dry out tomatoes** that are still fairly firm. If you can't use the sun, dry them in your oven on its lowest heat setting or use a dehydrator. Once dried, pop them in a jar and cover them with olive oil.

- **Roast tomatoes that** are going soft – they are great squashed onto toast!

PEPPERS

- Roast any wrinkly peppers and use them up in soups, pasta sauces, or whizz them into hummus (see p.20).

- Dice them and freeze for using later.

- Cut into thin slices and add them to a frittata.

CARROTS

- Grate carrots and use them to make fritters. Season and mix with beaten egg and flour before frying in a little oil. Try adding cumin and fresh coriander.

- Revive old carrots by slicing and steaming them, then add to a salad.

- Bake carrots that are past their prime in cakes and muffins (see p.66).

COURGETTES

- Grate or slice courgettes, toss lightly in oil, season to taste, then grill or roast until tender. Use in salads or sandwiches.

- Dice and add to soups, such as minestrone or Mediterranean vegetable.

BEETROOT

- Add grated beetroot to a chocolate cake or brownie mix for moistness and depth.

- Roast beets and blitz them with yogurt, garlic, and mint for a brightly coloured dip.

- Slice, steam, and toss into a salad. You can eat the leaves too!

Hero Hummus

Take snacking to a whole new level. OLD TOMATOES, EXTRA AVOCADO, *and* LEFTOVER BEANS *add a tasty waste-free twist to your hummus.*

MAKES ABOUT 330g (11½oz)

240g (8½oz) ready-to-eat chickpeas

1 large garlic clove, roughly chopped

1 tbsp nut or seed butter, such as almond or sunflower

½ tsp salt

2½ tbsp lemon juice

2–4 tbsp olive oil, plus extra to serve

1–2 tbsp filtered water (optional)

salt and freshly ground black pepper, to taste

To serve

1 tsp chopped fresh herb leaves and stalks, such as coriander or parsley (optional)

½ tsp paprika (optional)

1 tsp dukkah (optional)

FIRST MAKE THE BASE

1 Place the chickpeas, garlic, nut or seed butter, salt, lemon juice, and 2 tbsp of the olive oil in a food processor or blender and whizz until smooth. You may need to stop the motor occasionally and push the mixture back down with a spatula.

2 Add more olive oil and/or water to reach the desired consistency, if required.

3 Season with salt and pepper to taste, then drizzle with extra olive oil and sprinkle with herbs, paprika, and dukkah, if using.

4 Serve with some crunchy vegetables such as pepper or cucumber to dip, or store your hummus in an airtight container in the fridge for 3–4 days.

old tomatoes

LEFTOVER AVOCADO

Add **half a large avocado** at step 1 and whizz with the rest of the ingredients until smooth.

- - - - - - - - -

LEFTOVER BEANS

Swap the chickpeas for an **equal quantity of ready-to-eat beans**, such as soaked and cooked butter beans that you haven't used, or some leftover tinned cannellini beans.

- - - - - - - - -

OLD TOMATOES

Add about **60g (2oz) old tomatoes or leftover tomato tops and bottoms** at step 1, and whizz with the rest of the ingredients until smooth.

Leftover avocado

Leftover beans

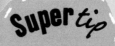

Super tip

Freeze for up to 4 months!

Eggs

Recipes often call for just one part of an egg but you can stop making your **WHITES, YOLKS, and SHELLS** *feel like spare parts by following these top tips. Soon you'll be using up* **EVERY LAST BIT!**

ADD SOME SHINE

Use your egg whites as a glaze for bread, muffins, and pastries. It adds a glossy sheen and helps to keep any grains, such as poppy or sesame seeds, in place on the crust.

THICKEN SOUPS

Adding egg yolks to soups and sauces gives them a smooth, velvety feel. Make sure to mix them in while the soup or sauce is fairly cool so that you don't end up with scrambled eggs.

DON'T HOLD THE MAYO!

Blitz your yolks with a hand blender, then very gradually drizzle in oil a few drops at a time while whisking constantly. This should take around 4 minutes. Add a squeeze of lemon juice or vinegar to taste.

STAIN REMOVAL

To clean a stained tea or coffee mug, simply grind up your eggshells, pop them in the mug, add some warm water, and leave to soak overnight. In the morning, the stains should have vanished!

FREEZE IT!

Freeze egg whites for up to 3 months. Once defrosted, use as normal.

Egg yolks dry out when stored but mixing a pinch of sugar or salt with each yolk before freezing will help. Label which are sweet or savoury, and adjust your recipe for any added sugar or salt.

GO NUTS!

Make candied nuts by whisking your egg whites with a little water. Mix in the nuts – almonds or pecans work well – then add cinnamon and sugar to taste. Bake on a tray in a low oven for around 1 hour, turning regularly, until crisp.

FROTH IT UP

Whisk up your whites and add them to your cocktails. They add froth and give your drinks a wonderfully silky texture.

EGGSHELL POWDER

Packed with micronutrients, eggshells are an awesome source of calcium! Use a small amount as a supplement – try adding ¼ tsp of powder to one large smoothie. You need about 20 eggshells to make half a small jar. Rinse well and remove any membrane before you start.

1 Preheat the oven to 180°C (350°F/ Gas 4). Bake the shells on a tray in the oven for 10 minutes.

2 Once the shells have cooled, blitz them in a food processor or grind with a pestle and mortar.

3 Keep grinding until you have a fine, powdery dust. Store in an airtight jar in the fridge for up to 3 weeks.

Save-it Soup

STALE BREAD, LEFTOVER GRAINS, or PASTA PIECES transform this hearty vegetable soup into a delicious zero-waste meal.

SERVES 4-6

1 tbsp olive oil, plus extra to serve

1 onion, finely chopped, about 100g (3½oz)

2 cloves garlic, crushed

1 carrot, finely chopped, about 100g (3½oz)

1 celery stick, finely chopped, about 75g (2½oz)

1 tsp dried rosemary

a generous pinch of chilli powder

400g (14oz) fresh tomatoes, chopped, or 400g can chopped tomatoes

1 courgette, finely chopped, about 150g (5½oz)

85g (3oz) kale leaves and stalks, finely chopped, tough stalks discarded

1–1.2 litres (1¾–2 pints) vegetable stock

salt and freshly ground black pepper, to taste

50g (1¾oz) Parmesan cheese, shaved (optional)

small handful basil leaves, to garnish

FIRST **MAKE THE BASE**

1 Heat the oil in a large, lidded pan on a low–medium heat.

2 Add the onion, garlic, carrot, celery, rosemary, and chilli powder, and cook gently for about 10 minutes with the lid askew, until the vegetables are soft.

3 Add the tomatoes, courgette, kale, and stock. Bring to the boil, then reduce the heat and continue to simmer, uncovered, for about 10 minutes.

4 Season with salt and pepper to taste. Serve with a drizzle of olive oil and Parmesan shavings (if using), and garnish with fresh basil.

Super tip
Keep a batch of base soup in the freezer so you always have something to add leftovers to.

LEFTOVER BEANS AND STALE BREAD

Add about **250g (9oz) leftover ready-to-eat beans**, such as cannellini or borlotti, at step 3, and top with **100g (3½oz) diced, dried bread "croutons"**, at step 4.

PARMESAN RINDS AND LEFTOVER PASTA

Add **2–3 leftover Parmesan cheese rinds** to the soup and **75g (2½oz) dried pasta** at step 3, making sure you follow the cooking time of the pasta. Alternatively, add **225g (8oz) leftover cooked pasta** towards the end of step 3 to heat through. Remove the rinds before serving.

LEFTOVER GRAINS OR PULSES

Add about **250g (9oz) leftover cooked grains or pulses,** such as buckwheat, brown rice, or lentils, to your soup towards the end of step 3. Heat through before serving.

Cake tin
clear-out

What can you do with the contents of your cake tin when it's starting to DRY OUT? From BAKING BISCOTTI to SHAKING IT UP, try these ideas to give your cakes a second take.

FREEZE IT!

Most cakes freeze well but avoid freezing cakes that have a cream or buttercream filling. Make sure your cake is cool, wrap it well in foil or clingfilm, and it should keep for a few months.

COOL TOPPING

Simply sprinkle your stale cake crumbs over ice-cream for a quick and easy dessert.

SPONGE LAYER

Dry cake makes a great base for sponge-based desserts, as it absorbs any fruity juices well.

BAKE BISCOTTI

Slice up old pieces of cake and bake them in the oven at 130°C (250°F/Gas ½) for around 50 minutes to make crunchy biscotti or sweet croutons.

SWEET CRUST

Dry your cake out completely by baking it on a low heat. Once cool, grind into crumbs and use to make a sweet pie crust, like a biscuit base.

CAKE REVIVAL

Revive stale cake by putting it in an airtight container with a slice of bread or apple overnight.

FRENCH TOAST CAKE

Cut thick slices of stale cake. Whisk up 3 eggs with 240ml (8fl oz) milk in a dish. Heat butter in a pan. Dip slices in the egg mix and fry on each side until golden.

CAKE SHAKE

Cake meets milkshake in this blended sweet treat. It's a neat way of using up old cake as the moisture from the milk more than compensates for any dryness.

— — — — — —

1 Break up dry slices of cake, such as fruit cake (see p.58), and crumble them into a food processor.

2 Pour in enough nut milk, such as almond milk (or see p.59), to cover the cake and blend until smooth.

3 Add a little more milk if you prefer a runnier shake and blend again. Sprinkle on cake crumbs to serve.

cake shake

Check it
before you chuck it

*knowing how to tell whether food is really **OFF** or whether it can still **BE SAVED** is not only **VITAL FOR YOUR HEALTH** but will also help you on your **ZERO-WASTE** quest!*

TEST YOUR MEAT

Smell meat to check whether it's safe to eat. Fresh meat should have little or no odour – if it smells putrid don't eat it! Check the texture. If meat is slimy or sticky, bin it. Colour is not a good guide as meats vary – changes in shade don't always mean that the meat is off.

TEST YOUR EGGS

To check an egg for freshness pop it into a glass of water. If it is fresh it will drop to the bottom and rest on its side. Standing on one end at the bottom means it's a bit old but fine to eat. However, if the egg floats to the surface you should throw it away.

FRESH

OK

DON'T EAT

Bad eggs float because they have air inside them – making them less dense than water

TEST YOUR BUTTER

To check whether your butter is fresh, cut a small slice from the block and look closely at the colour. The colour should be the same inside as on the outside. If the inside of the butter looks lighter it has oxidized and should be thrown away. You can always freeze butter if you aren't going to use it in time.

Colour should be the same inside and out

TEST YOUR OiL

Most rancid oils have a grassy or paint-like scent. Olive oil is an exception and smells like crayons when spoiled.

TEST YOUR FLOUR

Flour should have no smell at all. If your flour smells slightly sharp or bitter then it has gone off and you need to throw it away.

MOULD MATTERS

If you can see mould on the surface of food it means tiny fungi have penetrated deep inside. What you can see on top are only the spores, but their microscopic, threadlike roots will have spread throughout the food. Just scraping mould off the top will leave these roots behind. In general, this means you must throw the food away as some fungi can make you ill. However, there are a few exceptions, which are shown here.

✔ YOU CAN STILL EAT ...

Scrub off any mould

Cut away mould and 3cm (1in) around it

Cut away mould and at least 3cm (1in) below it

Dry-cured meat

Hard cheese

Hard fruit

Waste-free
Frittata

Make a meal out of your leftovers. This recipe breathes life into
VEG PEELINGS, SMOKED FISH *or leftover* **ROASTED VEG.**

SERVES 2-4

1 tbsp coconut or olive oil

1 onion, about 85g (3oz), finely chopped

3 garlic cloves, crushed

50g (1¾oz) spinach, tough stalks removed, chopped

100g (3½oz) broccoli florets, stem, and leaves, finely chopped

50g (1¾oz) peas, fresh or frozen

6 eggs

150ml (5fl oz) milk, nut or dairy

2 tbsp fresh chopped herbs such as parsley, dill, chives, or thyme

75g (2½oz) cheese, such as feta or Cheddar, crumbled or grated (optional)

salt and freshly ground black pepper

FIRST MAKE THE BASE

1 Heat the oil in a medium, non-stick, ovenproof frying pan over a medium heat.

2 Add the onion and garlic, and cook slowly for 3-4 minutes until soft.

3 Add the vegetables and cook for a further 4-5 minutes.

4 Whisk the eggs and milk together. Stir in the herbs and cheese, if using, then season with salt and pepper to taste.

5 Preheat the grill on a medium setting.

6 Level out the vegetables in the pan and gently pour the egg mixture over them. Reduce the heat to low-medium and continue to cook the frittata for 10-15 minutes, without stirring, until the underside is cooked.

7 Place the pan under the grill for about 5 minutes to set the top of the frittata.

8 Remove the frittata from the grill and allow to cool for 2-3 minutes before serving.

Super tip

Leftover frittata can be stored in the fridge for 1–2 days, and is delicious eaten cold.

VEG PEELINGS

Replace the spinach with 100g (3½oz) mixed vegetable peelings, such as carrot, beetroot, parsnip, or potato, and add to the frittata at step 3 with a splash of water. Increase the cook time at step 3 to 10 minutes.

SMOKED FISH

Add 150g (5½oz) of leftover ready-to-eat smoked fish, skinned and broken into bite-sized pieces, at step 6.

LEFTOVER ROASTED VEG

Replace the spinach, broccoli, and peas with around 300g (10oz) leftover cold roasted vegetables. Chop into small cubes if necessary, and add to the frittata at step 3.

Tops and tails

Don't bin those leftover bits of **VEGETABLES.** *Use them to* **ADD FLAVOUR** *to soup or* **MAKE STOCK** *— in fact the possibilities are endless!*

SHRED AND STIR

- **Finely chop broccoli** stalks, beetroot ends, and celery leaves, then add them to your stir-fries.

IT'S A WRAP

- **Use up tough** outer leaves of red cabbage by boiling them until they soften. They are great for wrapping food parcels or dumplings.

MASH IT UP

- **Chop and sauté** the tops of spring or green onions and add them to mashed potato for a big flavour boost.

SQUASHED!

- **Boil up any** squash flesh trimmings, then whizz into a purée for a side to serve with fish.
- **Roast pumpkin seeds** discarded from fresh pumpkins and use them as a nutritious garnish on salad.

MIND THAT RIND

• Watermelon rind can be added to smoothies or chopped up and added to stews to help bulk them out.

Super tip

Make stock by frying veg tops and tails in olive oil. Add water and herbs or spices of your choice. Bring to the boil and simmer for around 15 minutes before straining through a sieve.

HERBALICIOUS

• Herb stems - such as basil, coriander, and parsley – make a tasty addition to smoothies or chop them finely into soups and stews.

TOP SMOOTHIES

• Add strawberry tops to your smoothies for extra vitamins and fibre!

ADD SOME CRUNCH

• Liven up salads by adding crunchy raw broccoli stalks or cauliflower.

TIP TOP CARROTS

• Use green carrot tops in pesto (see p.40), or as a pretty garnish.

33

Lemons and limes

Are you tired of wasting the parts of your lemons and limes that your recipes don't call for? Think beyond adding a slice to your drinks, here's how to MAKE THE MOST of these flavoursome fruits...

ZINGY DRESSING

Squeeze lemon or lime juice straight onto salad leaves for an instant lift. Or try mixing lime juice with an equal amount of olive oil, a crushed garlic clove, then add honey to sweeten, and season to taste.

FROZEN SLICES

Slice up leftover lemons and limes, pop them onto a baking tray, and place in a freezer. Once frozen, transfer the slices to a freezer bag ready to put in your icy cold drinks!

DRIED SLICES

Place your lemon and lime slices on a cooling rack over a baking tray so that air can get to both sides. Put them in the oven at a low heat for around 2 hours until dry. Use them to flavour tea or chop them into soups.

LEMON MAYO

Adding both lemon zest and juice to mayonnaise gives it a zingy twist! Simply grate the zest into your mayo and/or squeeze in some juice, then mix it up.

CITRUS DUST

Use up citrus peel with this zesty powder. It tastes great sprinkled over chicken or fish. Dry peels in a dehydrator on its lowest setting for about 12 hours, or preheat your oven to a low heat (about 80°C/175°F/Gas ¼). You will need: 150g (5½oz) citrus peel, and a large pinch of salt (optional).

1 Spread the peels evenly in a single layer on a baking tray and bake for 2-3 hours until crisp and dry.

CITRUS INFUSION

Use leftover citrus peel to flavour spirits, such as vodka. Simply place the peel into the bottle of vodka and leave it to infuse.

2 Allow the dry peels to cool completely on the tray – this takes about 10 minutes.

3 Add the salt, if using, then whizz in a food processor or high-speed blender.

JUICE CUBES

When frozen, transfer cubes to a freezer bag. You can use them whenever you need to add fresh lemon or lime juice to a recipe. A cube should equal around 1 tbsp of juice.

4 Store the dust in an airtight container in the fridge for up to 3 months.

Rescue-it Risotto

Add COLD CUTS, LEFTOVER VEG, or ASPARAGUS STALKS to this store-cupboard risotto for a real supper saviour.

SERVES 2-3

1 tbsp coconut or olive oil, plus extra to serve

1 onion, finely chopped, about 100g (3½oz)

1 garlic clove, crushed

1 celery stick, finely chopped, about 75g (2½oz)

225g (8oz) risotto rice, Arborio or carnaroli

800ml-1 litre (1¼-1¾ pints) hot vegetable or chicken stock

60g (2oz) Parmesan cheese, grated

salt and freshly ground black pepper, to taste

1 tbsp chopped parsley, to garnish

¼-½ tsp chilli flakes, to garnish (optional)

FIRST MAKE THE BASE

1 Heat the oil in a large pan over a low-medium heat. Add the onion, garlic, and celery, and cook slowly, stirring occasionally, for about 5 minutes or until soft.

2 Add the rice and increase the heat to medium-high, stirring constantly for 1-2 minutes.

3 Add a ladleful of stock and stir until thoroughly absorbed into the rice.

4 Repeat this process a ladleful at a time, until the rice is creamy and tender, but still al dente. Depending on your rice, this will take 15-25 minutes, and the amount of stock needed will vary.

5 Remove the pan from the heat and stir in the Parmesan cheese.

6 Season to taste with salt and pepper. Place the lid on the pan and set aside for 2-3 minutes before serving.

7 Garnish with the parsley and chilli flakes, if using.

NOW ZERO-WASTE IT!

ASPARAGUS STALKS

Use up the whole of your asparagus spears. Take around **150g (5½oz) asparagus ends** and discard any parts that are very dry. Finely slice the rest into thin "coins". Stir into the risotto with the last ladleful of stock at step 4.

LEFTOVER ROAST CHICKEN

Shred about **150g (5½oz) cold, leftover chicken**, discarding the skin if necessary. Add to the risotto towards the end of step 4 to heat through.

LEFTOVER VEG-DRAWER VEG

Use up around **200g (7oz) leftover mixed veg** from your veg-drawer, such as carrots, peppers, or courgettes. Chop, and then steam in a steaming pan until cooked through. Add to the risotto towards the end of step 4 and continue as per the recipe.

Super tip
Mix all 3 variations for a zero-waste feast!

Grow it, don't throw it: lettuce

Don't bin those **LETTUCE ENDS!** The bases can be used to grow your very own **FRESH VEGETABLES** – a great way to make the most of your "waste". Follow these simple steps to get growing!

1 Chop off any leafy parts of your lettuce that you haven't already used so that just the root base remains. Pour a little warm water into a shallow bowl.

Super tip
Cabbage and celery can also be grown using this technique!

You only need the base of the lettuce head – you can eat the rest!

CHOP HERE!

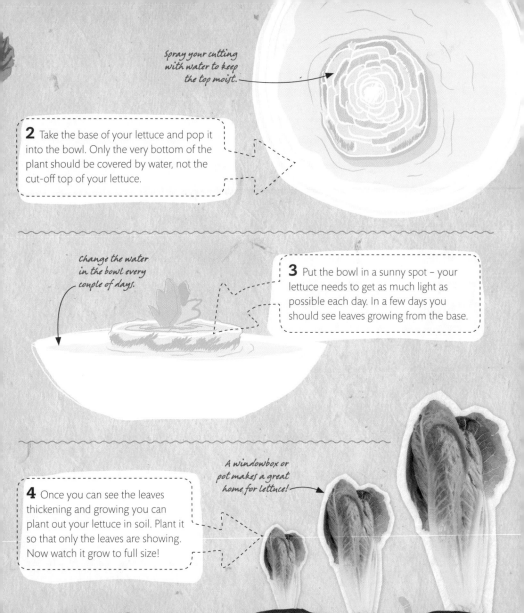

Spray your cutting
with water to keep
the top moist.

2 Take the base of your lettuce and pop it
into the bowl. Only the very bottom of the
plant should be covered by water, not the
cut-off top of your lettuce.

Change the water
in the bowl every
couple of days.

3 Put the bowl in a sunny spot – your
lettuce needs to get as much light as
possible each day. In a few days you
should see leaves growing from the base.

A windowbox or
pot makes a great
home for lettuce!

4 Once you can see the leaves
thickening and growing you can
plant out your lettuce in soil. Plant it
so that only the leaves are showing.
Now watch it grow to full size!

Pimp up your Pesto

For a pesto that still packs a punch, swap the traditional basil and pine nuts for **TIRED NUTS OR SEEDS, CARROT LEAVES,** *or* **LEFTOVER PARSLEY STALKS.**

MAKES ABOUT 160G (5½OZ)

2 cloves garlic, roughly chopped

65g (2oz) basil leaves, roughly chopped

50g (1¾oz) pine nuts

1 tbsp apple cider vinegar

4 tbsp olive oil

salt and freshly ground black pepper, to taste

FIRST MAKE THE BASE

1 Place the garlic, basil, pine nuts, and vinegar in a food processor and whizz until combined.

2 With the motor running, slowly drizzle the olive oil into the pesto until combined. You may need to stop the machine occasionally to push the mixture down with a spatula.

3 Season with salt and pepper to taste.

4 Store in an airtight container in the fridge for up to 1 week.

Super tip
Swap parsley stalks for wilting herbs such as mint or coriander.

Tired nuts or seeds

Carrot leaves

Leftover parsley stalks

NOW ZERO-WASTE iT!

TIRED NUTS OR SEEDS

Swap the pine nuts for 50g (1¾oz) **tired nuts or seeds**, such as walnuts or pumpkin seeds. Whizz them in the food processor before adding the other ingredients, then add an extra tbsp vinegar and an extra 2–4 tbsp olive oil. Adjust the oil as needed to get the right consistency.

- - - - - - - -

CARROT LEAVES

Swap the basil for 65g (2oz) thoroughly washed carrot leaves, plus an extra tbsp vinegar and an extra 2–4 tbsp olive oil. Carrot leaves are less juicy than basil, so adjust the amount of olive oil accordingly.

- - - - - - - -

LEFTOVER PARSLEY STALKS

Swap the basil for 65g (2oz) **leftover parsley stalks**, plus an extra tbsp vinegar and an extra 2–4 tbsp olive oil.

Bananas

Is your fruit bowl **BURSTING** with **BANANAS?** Don't let them turn black and end up in the bin. Try some of these **AWESOME IDEAS** to make the most of **EVERY BIT** of this fabulous fruit.

PERFECT PEEL!

Freeze banana peels ready to use them in baking cakes (see recipe p.59).

BUTTER IT UP

Squash overripe bananas onto toast or crumpets as a sweet swap for butter.

BANANAMOLE

Mash-up overripe bananas with avocado to bulk out your guacamole or even try replacing all the avocado with banana in your favourite guacamole recipe for a sweeter alternative.

FROZEN TREAT

Peel bananas, break into chunks, and freeze on a tray. Put in a freezer bag – add to smoothies as needed.

BANANA ICE CREAM

This easy-to-make but utterly delicious frozen treat makes a great healthy and vegan alternative to ice cream. Keep it simple with just one ingredient – a banana – or add any flavourings, such as berries or cocoa, that take your fancy.

1 Peel your banana – just use more bananas if you want to make a batch of ice cream – and chop into chunks.

2 Freeze the pieces for at least 2 hours then blitz in a food processor until smooth – try adding cocoa powder at this stage for chocolate flavoured "ice cream".

3 You can eat the ice cream right away or transfer to an airtight container and freeze it again to firm it up.

BANANA CHIPS

Slice up bananas that are fairly firm and use them to make chips. Make sure your slices are the same thickness, brush them with lemon juice, and pop them on a baking tray. Bake at 110°C (225°F/Gas ¼) for 2–3 hours until brown. Leave to cool and crisp.

Banana ice cream

MAKE IT MOIST

Add a ripe banana peel to the bottom of a roasting pan to help keep meat moist and tender while it cooks.

Love your leftovers...
Potatoes

Do your leftover potatoes leave you feeling as cold as **YESTERDAY'S MASH?** *Try these top tips and soon you'll be* **MAKING OVER** *your mash and* **REVIVING** *your roasts!*

Mashed

Shepherd's pie

TASTY TOPPING

Try using your mashed potato as a topping for pies instead of pastry. Spread the potato over your filling and pop it in the oven until warmed through and browning on top.

Fishcakes

POTATO PATTIES

Recycle your leftover mash into potato cakes by cracking in an egg, mixing it with the potato, and adding some herbs. Then form into patties or balls and fry off each side in a little oil until warmed through and crispy on the outside. Try adding cooked fish or bacon into the mix for extra flavour.

ADD THICKNESS

Mashed potato makes a great alternative to cornflour when it comes to thickening up your sauces, soups, or stews. Blend your leftover mash in a food processor until it is smooth – you may need to add a little milk or some of the dish you are thickening. Once it is smooth, gradually stir it into your soup or sauce until you reach the desired consistency.

Blending mashed potato thickens soup

Potato and bacon soup

Boiled

Roasted

Baked

SUPER SALAD

Boiled potatoes can be reworked into tasty potato salad. Cut the potatoes into bitesize pieces and mix up with mayonnaise, natural yogurt, boiled egg, peas, herbs, and chopped radishes – or whatever vegetables you have to hand!

JUST ADD EGGS

Leftover roast potatoes make a great addition to a frittata (see pp.30–31) or Spanish omelette. Whisk up 3 or 4 eggs with a little water and seasoning. Fry off a sliced onion in a little oil over a medium heat until golden, slice your potatoes, then add them to the pan. Pour in the egg mix and reduce heat. Let the omelette cook through for around 12 minutes.

STUFFED SPUDS

Give baked potatoes a new lease of life by mixing up the flesh with flavourful fillings. Slice your baked potatoes in half and scoop out the flesh. Place it in a bowl with fillings of your choice. Mix it all together and season to taste. Stuff the filling into the potato skin, sprinkle on some grated cheese and bake in the oven until warmed through and the top has browned.

Fresh herbs liven up potato salad

Crispy, golden topping

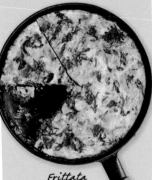

Frittata

Cheese and bacon

45

Creative
Crisps

Transform **POTATO PEELINGS** *or* **OLD VEG** *into these moreish crisps. A healthy snack from leftover veg!*

SERVES 2

50g (1¾oz) potato peel from around 2 large potatoes

½ tbsp olive oil

a generous pinch of chilli powder

½ tsp sweet smoked paprika powder

¼ tsp salt

freshly ground black pepper, to taste

50g (1¾oz) kale leaves

FIRST **MAKE THE BASE**

1 Preheat the oven to 150°C (300°F/Gas 2) and line 2–3 baking trays with baking parchment.

2 Place the potato peel in a mixing bowl with half of the oil, spices, salt, and pepper. Using your hands (wear gloves if necessary), gently rub the peel until it is completely coated with oil and spices. Set aside.

3 Using a sharp knife, remove the tough, woody kale stems and roughly chop the leaves into bite-sized pieces.

4 Place the kale in a mixing bowl with the remaining oil, spices, salt, and pepper. Gently rub the kale for 1–2 minutes until it is completely coated and starting to soften.

5 Spread the potato peel and kale thinly on separate baking trays in single, even layers. Set the kale tray aside.

6 Place the potato peel in the oven and leave to roast for 25 minutes. After 10 minutes, add the kale tray and continue roasting for the remaining 15 minutes, or until crisp. Watch carefully to ensure they don't burn.

7 Remove the crisps from the oven and leave on the trays for a few minutes to crisp up before eating.

8 The crisps are best eaten within a few hours, but can be stored in an airtight container for 1–2 days. Re-crisp them in the oven at a low temperature for 3–4 minutes.

NOW ZERO-WASTE IT!

SWEET POTATO AND POTATO PEEL CRISPS

Swap the kale for the peel of 2 large sweet potatoes – about 50g (1¾oz). Combine with the regular potato peel and season as per the recipe. Roast both for 25 minutes, or until crisp.

TIRED PARSNIP AND POTATO PEEL CRISPS

Swap the kale for 1 parsnip – about 100g (3½oz). Slice very thinly either with a mandolin or a veg peeler, including tops and tails. Season, spread thinly on a baking tray, and roast for around 35 minutes, or until crisp. Thicker slices may need an extra 5 minutes, but watch carefully to ensure they don't burn. Add the potato peel tray to the oven for the last 25 minutes.

TIRED BEETROOT AND POTATO PEEL CRISPS

Swap the kale for 1 beetroot – about 100g (3½oz). Slice very thinly either with a mandolin or a veg peeler, including tops and tails. Season, spread thinly on a baking tray, and roast for around 35 minutes, or until crisp. Thicker slices may need an extra 5 minutes, but watch carefully to ensure they don't burn. Add the potato peel tray to the oven for the last 25 minutes.

Everything
in its place!

Knowing whether to put your food in the CUPBOARD, FREEZER, or FRIDGE will help it last longer and reduce waste. LABEL FOODS so you know what will go off when. Track what you use and what you waste.

Fridge

Check up on your refrigerated foods regularly and move older foods to the front so that you use them up before newer foods. Label anything that is going off as a reminder to use it soon! Knowing exactly what is in your fridge means you can avoid buying duplicates.

The warmest part of your fridge is the door, so use it for items that are less sensitive to temperature. Bottles or jars of condiments and cartons of juice do well here.

The top shelf of your fridge has the most consistent temperature and anything that is ready to eat, like dairy products and cooked meat, should be kept here.

Don't store cheese in plastic wrap – it needs to breathe. It will last longer in wax paper.

For freshness, keep red spices, like paprika and chilli, in the fridge in airtight tins or jars.

Raw foods that will need to be cooked, like meat and fish, should be stored on the bottom shelf of the fridge so that they can't drip onto anything.

Peppers and lettuce are best kept in a plastic bag in the salad drawer.

Super tip

Put mushrooms in a paper bag in the fridge to stop them going slimy.

Cupboard

Your cupboard is the best place for jars of dried foods, and bottles of oil or vinegar that don't need to be chilled but do need to be cool, dry, and dark.

Freezer

The golden rule for freezing food is to label everything! On the label, make sure you include what kind of food it is and the date you made or bought it. Arrange your freezer so that the label faces outward with older foods towards the front. This means that you won't have to rummage around and mess up all your neat work.

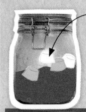

To stop brown sugar going hard, keep it in an airtight container and add moist foods like a slice of bread or marshmallows for 1–2 days. The sugar will soften as it soaks up any moisture.

Vacuum sealing leftovers before you freeze them can save valuable freezer space and it helps prevent freezer-burn. Another waste-saving tip is to freeze food by serving size so you only defrost what you need and don't end up with leftovers.

Arrange your cupboard by grouping like items together so that you can find them quickly and keep an eye on what you have in stock. It's useful to label anything that is coming to the end of its shelf-life and needs to be used soon. Storing items in clear, glass, airtight containers allows you to see exactly how much you have.

Shop smart!

*Stop before you shop! Take time to plan **WHAT** you need, **WHERE** you should buy it, and **HOW MUCH** to get in one go — without wasting it.*

LEARN TO LiST

A shopping list is essential for ensuring you don't buy more food than you need. Whether you stick to a strict meal plan or have a looser guide (see p.14), use your weekly menu as the basis for your shopping list. Check what ingredients you already have and list anything extra you'll need along with the quantities required. Once you're out shopping, stick to your list and don't let special offers tempt you off-plan!

Build your list from your meal plan.

WHERE TO SHOP

Supermarkets are convenient for buying everything under one roof, but your local farmers' market has its advantages. Local produce is fresher as it has travelled less far and it comes with less packaging – you can even hand back any ties or bands on the produce to the stallholder. So make an effort to buy your perishable goods locally at the market. They often sell imperfect veg that supermarkets refuse, so you also may find that shopping here is cheaper.

Fruit and veg market

Don't forget your reusable bag when you head to the shops!

BARGAIN BEWARE!

Don't be tempted by what might look like great bargain buys. Shops discount fresh produce that is near or at its use-by date but unless you're sure you will use it all right away, you will end up wasting it. Try to buy loose veg where you can and select the exact number you need rather than opting for cheap multipacks, or you may end up throwing away more than you use!

Bags of salad go off quickly, so note the dates.

Pick the exact amount of veg you need.

BUYING IN BULK

Buying large quantities of food in one go is cheaper, reduces packaging, and the number of shopping trips you make. But only bulk-buy foods that will keep long enough for you to use them. Good foods to buy in bulk include: dried beans, rice, oats, pasta, nuts, dried fruit and condiments you use often. When decanting bulk buys don't top-up containers, make sure you remove any remaining food first and put it back on the top so that it gets used next.

Super tip

Clearly label the containers you store your bulk buys in with the use-by dates.

Store all your bulk buys in airtight jars for freshness.

Brown rice   Buckwheat   Lentils   Flaked almonds

Peanuts   Hazelnuts   Almonds   Raisins   Brazil nuts   Walnuts   Dried figs   Dates

Frugal
Flapjacks

Add a fruity twist to your flapjacks with **OVERRIPE BERRIES,**
CITRUS PEEL, or even **LEFTOVER PULP** *from your juicer.*

SERVES 12–16

100g (3½oz) coconut oil

150g (5½oz) honey
or rice syrup

150g (5½oz) nut or seed
butter

200g (7oz) rolled oats

100g (3½oz) flaked almonds

50g (1¾oz) ground almonds

1 tbsp ground cinnamon

100g (3½oz) mixed dried
fruit, such as dates, raisins,
figs, or goji berries, chopped

200g (7oz) mixed seeds,
such as pumpkin, sunflower,
chia, sesame, or hemp

FIRST **MAKE THE BASE**

1 Preheat the oven to 180°C (350°F/Gas 4) and line
a 30 x 20cm (12 x 8in) baking tray with baking parchment.

2 Gently heat the oil, honey, and nut or seed butter in a
pan until combined.

3 Mix all the other ingredients in a large bowl.

4 Pour the honey mixture over the oats and stir until
thoroughly combined.

5 Turn the flapjack mixture into the baking tray and
level out, pressing down firmly with the back of a spoon.
Bake for 25–30 minutes until golden brown.

6 Leave the flapjack in the tray on a wire rack to cool
completely before slicing.

7 Store in an airtight container in the fridge for up to
1 week, or freeze for up to 1 month.

OVERRIPE BERRIES

Heat **150g (5½oz) berries**, such as **blueberries or raspberries**, and **1 tbsp water** in a saucepan over a medium heat for about 5 minutes, until soft. Mash with a fork, then add the oil, honey, and nut or seed butter.

SATSUMA, TANGERINE, OR MANDARIN PEEL

Add the **finely chopped peel** of a piece of **citrus fruit (about 2 tbsp)** at step 2.

LEFTOVER JUICING PULP

There are endless flavour possibilities from whatever you used in your juice! Add **150g (5½oz) juicing pulp** to the honey mixture at step 1, combine, then continue as per the recipe.

Super tip

Eat them raw!
Instead of baking,
freeze for 1 hour,
then store in
the fridge.

I'm raw!

One-meal wonder

Find out just how far ONE MEAL can go with these awesome ideas for making the MOST of your ROAST.

Sunday:
The big dinner

You've cooked a roast chicken dinner but what can you do with the leftover meat, potatoes, and accompanying vegetables? And how long will they keep before they spoil? Cooked meat keeps for around three to four days and vegetables for up to five days if refrigerated. Store both in airtight containers in the fridge.

Roast chicken dinner

Day 1
Monday:

Lunch
VEGETABLE FRITTERS

Use up any leftover cooked veg by shredding them into a bowl with a little grated cheese. Season and mix well. Stir in an egg and combine. Fry off spoonfuls of the mix in olive oil, over a medium heat, for a couple of minutes on each side or until crisp.

Dinner
ROAST CHICKEN STIR-FRY

Add leftover roasted chicken to your stir-fry mix. Make sure it is thoroughly heated through before serving.

Day 2

Tuesday:

Lunch
SALAD WiTH POTATO CROUTONS

Give texture to your salad by adding roast potato croutons. Simply take the potatoes out of the fridge and allow them to come back to room temperature – or refry for extra crunch. Then crumble them over your salad.

Dinner
CHiCKEN TACOS

Shred your leftover chicken and fry it in a little oil along with taco spices and seasoning of your choice. Warm tortillas in a pan and spoon in your spicy chicken. Add toppings, such as cheese, sour cream, beans, salsa, and lettuce.

Day 3

Wednesday:

Lunch
BUBBLE & SQUEAK

Mix all your veg in a bowl (chop up any large chunks of potato) and season. Heat some butter or oil in a pan and fry the mix over a medium heat for around 10 minutes, turning frequently, until crisp and browned throughout. Serve with scrambled egg and grilled tomato.

Dinner
CHiCKEN, VEG, & PASTA BAKE

Stir bite-size chunks of leftover roast chicken into your mix for a vegetable and pasta bake before putting it in the oven.

10 FREEZE

foods you didn't know you could...

NUTS

With their high oil content, nuts such as pecans, almonds, and walnuts are prone to going rancid, which can be a problem when buying in bulk. Freeze them – either in their shells or shelled – and they will last at least twice as long.

KEEPS FOR 1-2 YEARS

OPENED WINE

Freeze any leftover wine in ice cube trays, transfer the cubes to freezer bags, and then pop them into sauces, stews, or risottos straight from the freezer.

KEEPS FOR 6 MONTHS

HARD CHEESES

Never let an old block of cheese moulder away at the back of the fridge again! It's best to grate it first, so that you can grab handfuls as you need them, and store it in an airtight bag or container.

KEEPS FOR 6 MONTHS

FRESH HERBS

If a recipe calls for just a sprig or two of fresh herbs, what do you do with the rest of the bunch? Freeze it of course! Place unneeded fresh herbs in an ice cube tray, cover with a little water, leave to freeze, then transfer to freezer bags.

KEEPS FOR 6 MONTHS

MASHED POTATOES

If you've got a bag of potatoes past their prime, make a large batch of mash and freeze individual portions for later. Use the same method for sweet potato or swede, too.

KEEPS FOR 2 MONTHS

Making friends with your **FREEZER** is a great way to avoid food waste. If you're buying in **BULK** to cut down on **PACKAGING**, freezing your produce will ensure it doesn't go off before you can use it.

Super tip
Glass jars are great for freezing foods and can be recycled (unlike plastic bags or wrap). Leave space for the contents to expand.

EGGS

You can store raw egg in the freezer – but not whole eggs, which may expand and crack. Either whisk in a bowl and pour the mixture into an ice cube tray or, if you're a keen baker, why not freeze the whites and yolks separately?

KEEPS FOR 1 YEAR

COOKED PASTA

Freezing is a great way to preserve any leftover cooked pasta. Make sure you cook it al dente, otherwise it may go mushy when you defrost it.

KEEPS FOR 2 MONTHS

CAKE

You can freeze cake as long as it doesn't have any icing, filling, or decoration. Either freeze it whole or cut it into slices and store them individually. Freezing cake also reduces the crumbs around the edges, making it easier to ice.

KEEPS FOR 6 MONTHS

UNCOOKED BROWN RICE

Brown rice has a higher natural oil content than white rice, so its shelf life is much shorter. The simple solution? Freeze it in a sealed, airtight container.

KEEPS FOR 6 MONTHS

DICED VEGETABLES

Dice fresh onions, peppers, or chillies, and freeze them flat in freezer bags. Press "score lines" into the bags before they have fully frozen so that you can break off individual portions.

KEEPS FOR 1 MONTH

Fruity Cake

Choose **BANANA PEELS, PINEAPPLE CORES,** *or* **NUT MILK PULP** *to turn up the flavour in this wonderful waste-free treat.*

MAKES 8-12 SLICES

60g (2oz) coconut oil

150g (5½oz) maple syrup

1 tsp vanilla extract

140g (5oz) chickpea, brown rice, or wholemeal flour

140g (5oz) ground almonds

1 tbsp baking powder

1 tsp cinnamon

50g (1¾oz) walnuts, chopped

250g (9oz) mixed dried fruit, such as apricots, prunes, raisins, figs, or dates, chopped

3 eggs, separated

100ml (3½fl oz) fresh orange juice (about 2 large oranges)

1 tbsp flax seeds

FIRST MAKE THE BASE

1 Preheat the oven to 180°C (350°F/Gas 4), and grease and line a 20cm (8in) round cake tin, or 900g (2lb) loaf tin.

2 Place the coconut oil, syrup, and vanilla in a small saucepan. Melt over a medium heat, then set aside to cool.

3 In a large mixing bowl, combine the flour, almonds, baking powder, cinnamon, walnuts, and dried fruit.

4 Separate the egg yolks from the whites. Whisk the whites until they form soft peaks, and set aside.

5 Add the orange juice to the cooled syrup mixture, then gently beat in the egg yolks.

6 Pour the syrup mix into the flour mixture and stir until thoroughly combined. Very gently, fold in the egg whites with a spatula.

7 Pour the cake mix into the tin. Level out and sprinkle with flax seeds.

8 Bake the cake for 50–60 minutes, or until golden brown, firm to the touch, and a skewer inserted into the centre comes out clean.

9 Leave the cake to cool in the tin for 5 minutes. Turn out onto a wire rack, and allow to cool completely before serving. Store in an airtight container for up to 1 week.

Super tip

Save the eggshells to make Eggshell Powder as on p.22.

NOW ZERO-WASTE iT!

BANANA PEEL

Swap the dried fruit and juice for **250g (9oz) topped, tailed, and roughly chopped ripe banana peels** (about 4–6 peels). Whizz in a food processor or blender with **100ml (3½fl oz) water** until smooth and dark. Combine with the syrup mixture and egg yolks at step 5.

PINEAPPLE RINGS AND CORES

Replace the mixed dried fruit with about **150g (5½oz) thinly sliced, skinned pineapple rings, with cores**. Replace the orange juice with **pineapple juice** and omit the flax seeds. Put the rings at the bottom of the baking tin and pour the cake mixture on top. Serve the cake upside-down with the baked pineapple on top.

LEFTOVER NUT MILK PULP

Swap the ground almonds for an **equal amount of very thoroughly squeezed nut milk pulp**, such as almond or hazelnut pulp (see below), and continue as per the recipe.

Nut milk

To make nut milk, soak **150g (5½oz) nuts** overnight in double their volume of water, then drain and rinse. Place in a blender or processor with **750ml (1¼ pints) filtered water** and whizz for 30–60 seconds. Strain the milk through muslin into a jug.

Know when to throw: fruit and veg

Learn when your FRUIT and VEGETABLES can be RESCUED or when they are past the point of no return and destined for COMPOST.

VILE VEG!

Take a look at your vegetables. If they are a bit dry or limp they can be rescued but if they are mushy, slimy, or discoloured they are rotten and you should discard them. Some veg behaves differently when it goes bad.

LOSE THAT BRUISE

While mushiness and wrinkles signal that your fruit is no longer good to eat, bruised fruit can be salvaged. Bruises are caused by damage in transport or handling rather than spoilage. Simply cut away the bruised part and then enjoy the rest of the fruit.

Cut away bruise

Celery becomes white and hollow

Aubergines toughen up and skin dimples

Asparagus tips go soft and turn black

Bad apples may smell sour

FOUL FRUIT!

To check whether soft fruits can be saved you need to examine their skins. The skins of fruits like apricots, plums, and grapes should be smooth not wrinkled or peeling away.

When fruit is going off it tends to start smelling bad, so ditch any fruits with a foul odour.

Give hard fruits, such as melons, a squeeze. They should be quite firm with no squashy areas. Check the skin for any dark patches, which develop when the fruit is off.

Fresh apricots have smooth skin

Melons should have no squashy patches

SAVE YOUR GREENS

Leafy greens can wilt within a couple of days but this doesn't always mean you have to bin them. Soak stems in warm water for around 10–15 minutes. If this doesn't revive them then pop them in the compost.

REVIVED

COMPOST

Love your leftovers...
Rice

Treat your rice right and don't let it end up in the BIN. With a little care you can reuse it in some of these TASTY DISHES.

COLD RICE

YES YOU CAN

REHEAT RICE

Worried about reheating rice? It is safe to heat up leftover rice the next day so long as you have kept it in the fridge and not left it out overnight. Once you have cooked rice you should chill it as soon as possible and keep it cool in the fridge until you want to use it.

PERFECT PUDDING

Leftover cooked rice is perfect for rice pudding. Cover the rice with milk in a pan and stir over a medium heat until it boils, then reduce the heat. Sweeten with honey or maple syrup. Add more milk if you like your pudding less solid. Keep stirring until the rice is soft and you have the consistency desired.

SIMPLE SALAD

You can add pretty much anything to your chilled leftover rice to make a delicious salad. Try mixing with leftover roasted vegetables, tuna, or cooked beans for a quick and healthy lunch. Chop in some fresh herbs and add a squeeze of lemon juice to give it a lift.

+ sugar & cinnamon

+ fruit & spices

+ fruit compote

CRISP CRUST

Cooked rice (shortgrain works best) makes a great alternative to a pastry for crusty toppings or bases for pies and quiches. Mix your leftover rice with some grated cheese and egg white then press together to form a crust. Or spray a pie dish with oil, and press the mix on to the bottom and sides of the dish. Bake in the oven until firm, then cool before filling.

Tomato and Dijon tart

Crispy rice and Parmesan base

GET STUFFED

Try stuffing vegetables – such as peppers, courgettes, or large tomatoes – with your leftover rice. Slice the top off the peppers (keep them to use as lids once they are stuffed) and remove the seeds. Scoop out courgette or tomato flesh and chop it up. Mix it with the rice, some herbs, feta cheese, and seasoning before spooning the mixture into the veg. Roast the stuffed vegetables in a little olive oil for 20–30 minutes at 160°C (325°F/Gas 3).

Stuffed peppers

Stringy mozzarella oozes in the middle

Arancini

RISOTTO BALLS

Use up leftover risotto by making arancini (fried rice balls). A gooey mozzarella centre is a must, so chop some into chunks. Take your chilled risotto and roll it in your hands to form a ball about 5cm (2in) across. Poke a hole in the centre, push in some mozzarella and any other fillings of your choice. Next, roll the ball in some flour, dip it in beaten egg, and coat with breadcrumbs. Fry the ball in olive oil until crisp and golden all over.

Rice salad

Bread bin
clear-out

*Bread is one of the foods we **THROW AWAY** most. Buck the trend by trying out some of these tasty tips.*

BREAD REVIVAL

Bring bread that is past its best back to life by freshening it up in the oven. Pre-heat your oven to 150°C (300°F/Gas 2) then sprinkle the crust of your bread with a little water. Bake the bread for around 8–10 minutes, depending on the size of the loaf, or until warmed through and the crust is crisped.

SOAK IT UP

Stale bread makes a handy sponge for drawing up excess fat. Put a slice on top of oily gravy, soups, or stews for a few seconds and it will soak up any unwanted grease. Discard the bread once it's soaked.

FRY IT OFF

An easy way to use up dry bread is to simply fry it or toast it. For a tasty brunch, try making French toast. Whisk up an egg, a few drops of vanilla extract, and a pinch of cinnamon in a shallow dish. Next stir in a little milk. Dip the stale bread into the mixture, making sure both sides are coated. Fry in a little oil or butter over a medium heat until golden brown on each side.

OH CRUMBS!

Fresh bread is not good for making breadcrumbs but older, dry bread is perfect. Avoid bread that is truly stale as it will make stale-tasting crumbs.

1 Make your breadcrumbs in a food processor or use a grater. Simply cut off the crusts then blitz or grate the bread into crumbs. Breadcrumbs made in a food processor are usually finer and more uniform in size than the grated ones.

2 Freeze your breadcrumbs – put them into an airtight container in the freezer and they should keep for up to two months.

3 Use your breadcrumbs to make everything from meatballs to veggie sausages, or mixed with cheese, herbs and spices as a tasty topping for vegetables or chicken.

CRUNCHY CROUTONS

Use stale bread to make croutons. Slice and remove crusts, then brush both sides with olive oil. Break or slice into bite-size chunks or cubes. Bake in the oven at 180°C (350°F/Gas 4) for about 20 minutes or until golden brown. Leave to cool before adding to soups or salads. Croutons can be stored in an airtight container for up to two weeks or frozen for up to a month.

EXTRA THICK

Add bulk and texture to soups by adding stale bread. Cut the crusts off the bread and tear it into chunks. Add the chunks to your soup and simmer for a few minutes to let the bread break down. Your soup should thicken up instantly.

Waste-not Want-not Muffins

Choose **TIRED SWEET POTATO, BEETROOT,** *or* **COURGETTE,** *and add* **WILTING HERBS** *to make these muffins your own.*

SERVES 12

115g (4oz) coconut or olive oil, plus extra for greasing

285g (10oz) chickpea, buckwheat, brown rice, or wholemeal flour

1 tbsp baking powder

½ tsp salt

2 eggs

235ml (8fl oz) milk, either nut or dairy

2 tbsp finely chopped parsley

2 spring onions, including green tops, finely chopped (about 3-4 tbsp)

freshly ground black pepper, to taste

150g (5½oz) carrot, grated (about 2 carrots)

50g (1¾oz) cheese such as Cheddar, feta, or Parmesan, grated or crumbled (optional)

FIRST **MAKE THE BASE**

1 Preheat the oven to 200°C (400°F/Gas 6) and grease a 12-hole muffin tin with a little oil.

2 If using coconut oil, melt it in a saucepan over a medium heat, and set aside to cool.

3 Combine the flour, baking powder, and salt in a mixing bowl, then set aside.

4 Lightly whisk the eggs and milk together, then stir in the parsley and onions. Add the oil and season with pepper to taste.

5 Pour the egg mixture into the flour mixture and stir until thoroughly combined, then fold in the carrot and cheese, if using.

6 Divide the mixture evenly between the muffin holes and bake for 15–20 minutes until golden brown and a skewer inserted into the centre comes out clean.

7 Leave the muffins to cool in the tray for 5 minutes, then run a knife round each muffin to loosen before turning out onto a wire rack.

8 These muffins are best eaten warm, but can be stored in an airtight container in the fridge for up to 1 week. Reheat in the oven at 150°C (300°F/Gas 2) for 5 minutes before serving, if desired.

TIRED SWEET POTATO AND THYME

Swap the carrot for grated sweet potato (with skin on), and the parsley for thyme, or any other wilting herbs that need using up.

— — — — —

TIRED BEETROOT AND CORIANDER

Swap the carrot for grated beetroot (with skin on), and the parsley for coriander, or any other wilting herbs that need using up.

— — — — —

TIRED COURGETTE AND MINT

Swap the carrot for grated courgette (with skin on), and the parsley for mint, or any other wilting herbs that need using up.

Super tip
keeping the skin on your veg adds extra nutrients.

It's more
than Food!

Think beyond leftovers and veg peelings – you may waste more than just food in your kitchen. From FOIL and FOOD WRAPS to PLASTIC BAGS and PACKAGING, here are some tips to cut your non-food kitchen waste.

FOiLED!

There's no need to use disposable aluminium foil, when there are reusable alternatives. Try silicone baking mats instead of foil sheets. If you do use them, clean aluminium foil wrap and trays can usually be recycled.

Foil trays

ZAP iT!

Don't bin your old kitchen sponges. Revive them and kill any lingering bacteria by soaking them and zapping them in the microwave for a couple of minutes. Don't attempt this with sponges that contain any metal, such as heavy-duty scourers.

Kitchen sponge

Foil sheet

ON TAP

Don't buy bottled water when you can drink water from your kitchen tap. Use glass bottles or jugs if you prefer your water chilled from the fridge. If you are concerned about water quality in your area, consider investing in a counter-top filter.

GADGET ADDICT

Think before you buy the latest kitchen gadget – do you really need it and will you use it? For example, spiralizers are great fun but your vegetable peeler produces similar results.

Use a peeler to make vegetable ribbons

IT'S A COVER UP

Avoid clingfilm by making your own reusable cloth covers for jars, plates, and bowls. You can use old cotton shirts or sheets to make these truly zero-waste! Simply cut circles out of the cloth, making sure they are around 5cm (2in) larger in diameter than the items you want to cover. Then gather the edge and stitch in some elastic. Now you're covered!

This is the size of the top of the jar or bowl

Add 5cm (2in) extra all around the edge

food cover

BULK UP!

Buying large quantities of food, such as dry goods like rice and flour that you can store, reduces packaging overall. This works out cheaper so is easy on your pocket and it means fewer shopping trips, saving you time! Look out for shops that specialize in bulk buying, allowing you to bring your own reusable containers to fill with food.

Courgette ribbons

Reusable containers mean less packaging

A fabric bag can be used over and over

Rice

IN THE BAG

Ditch wasteful plastic carrier bags and replace them with durable fabric totes. To avoid getting caught short, keep your reusable bags by the door, in the car, or pop a fold-up mini shopping bag in your pocket or handbag.

Grow it, don't throw it: potatoes

Did you know that you can GROW your own POTATOES from OLD SPUDS and the SCRAPS that you usually throw away? Follow these simple steps and you'll be HARVESTING SPUDS for months to come!

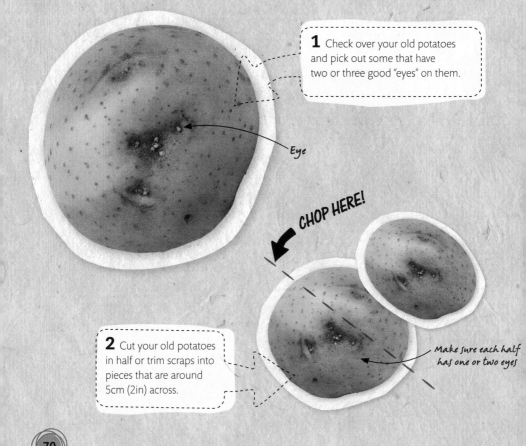

1 Check over your old potatoes and pick out some that have two or three good "eyes" on them.

Eye

CHOP HERE!

2 Cut your old potatoes in half or trim scraps into pieces that are around 5cm (2in) across.

Make sure each half has one or two eyes

70

3 Leave your potato halves or scraps out to dry, preferably overnight, or until they are dry to the touch.

Turn the potato around so the eyes are on top

4 Plant the potato pieces about 20cm (8in) deep in soil with the eyes facing up. Leave around 30cm (1ft) between your potatoes.

30cm (1ft) between each potato

Shoots will begin to grow from the eyes

5 In a few weeks' time you should see your potato plant start to grow!

New potatoes are ready in 10–12 weeks, larger varieties in 20–26 weeks

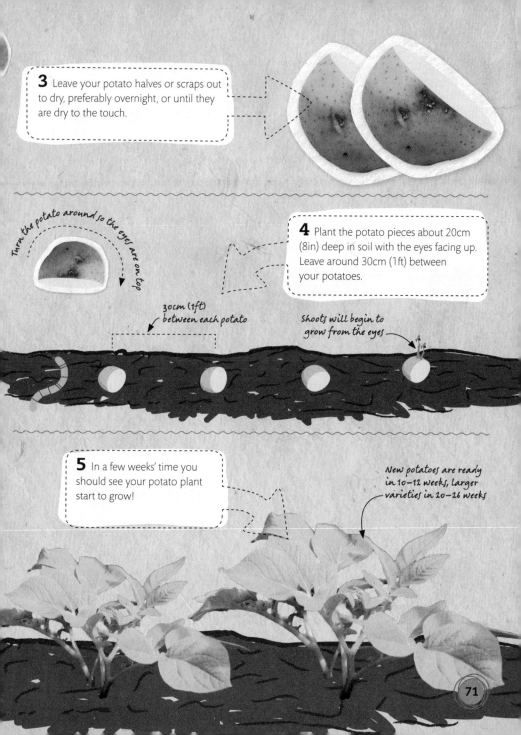

71

Index

Acknowledgments

Kate Turner has been creating deliciously healthy food for herself and her family for years. She has a degree in health sciences, is a recipe writer, magazine contributor, and author. Her DK publications include *Energy Bites*, *Superfood Breakfasts*, and *Power Bowls*. Kate shares ideas about food and family life on her blog **homegrownkate.com**.

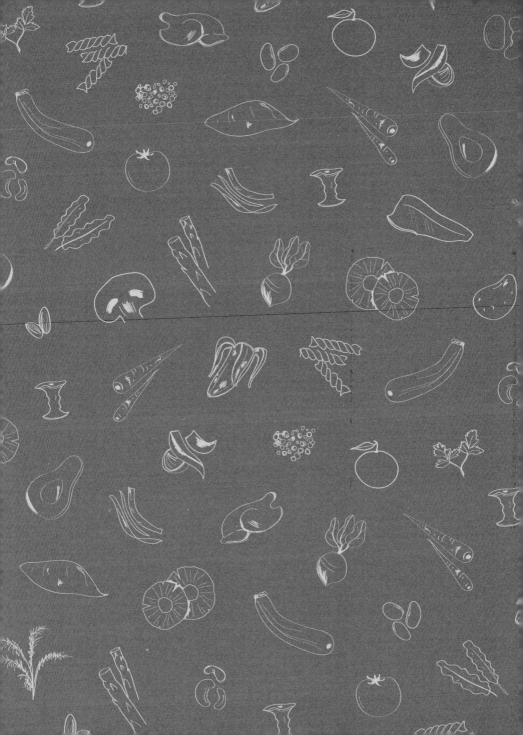